UKULELE
LEARN TO PLAY ANYWHERE & ANYTIME

RON MANUS • L. C. HARNSBERGER

DiY is an interactive multimedia experience—with video and audio demonstrations available for every lesson, example, and song in the book. You can stream or download corresponding media to your computer or mobile device wherever you see . Simply follow along in the book, and you will have everything you need.

To access the accompanying media, go to **alfred.com/redeem** and enter the code found on the inside front cover of this book.

Alfred Music
P.O. Box 10003
Van Nuys, CA 91410-0003
alfred.com

ISBN-10: 1-4706-1137-6 (Book & Media)
ISBN-13: 978-1-4706-1137-8 (Book & Media)

Ukulele photo courtesy of C.F. Martin & Company
Gears: © iStockphoto / aleksandarvelasevic • Blueprint: © iStockphoto / Branislav

 Alfred Cares. Contents printed on environmentally responsible paper.

CONTENTS
DO IT YOURSELF: UKULELE

Selecting Your Ukulele 3

The Parts of Your Ukulele............................4

How to Hold Your Ukulele............................5

   Standing 5

   Sitting 5

The Right Hand: Strumming the Strings 6

   Strumming with a Pick.................................6

   Strumming with Your Fingers 6

Using Your Left Hand 7

   Hand Position...7

   Placing a Finger on a String.......................7

How to Tune Your Ukulele 8

   Tuning with the Online Media 9

   Tuning the Ukulele to Itself 9

   Pitch Pipes and Electronic Tuners 9

Getting Acquainted with Music 10

   The Staff 10

   Measures 10

   Clefs 10

Reading TAB...11

Chord Diagrams...11

The First String A...12

     Playing with A, B, and C 12

     Extra Credit.......................................13

Sound-Off: How to Count Time 14

   Four Kinds of Notes...................................14

   Time Signatures 14

Repeat Signs 15

     1st String Blues....................................15

The Second String E.......................................16

     Jammin' on Two Strings.....................16

     Hot Cross Buns 17

     Blues in C..18

     Rockin' Uke...19

The Third String C 20

     Jammin' on Three Strings...................20

     Largo 21

     Jingle Bells 22

     Beautiful Brown Eyes 23

Introducing B-Flat 24

     Aura Lee 24

     Three-String Boogie 25

Tempo Signs 26

   Quarter Rest 26

     Three-Tempo Rockin' Uke.....................26

The C7 Chord...27

The F Chord...28

     Good Night Ladies.................................29

Key Signatures...30

   Ties 30

     Down in the Valley...............................30

     Ode to Joy 32

The C Chord...33

Incomplete Measures 34

     A-Tisket, A-Tasket................................34

Eighth Notes...35

     Jammin' with Eighth Notes...................35

Dotted Quarter Notes 36

     Cockles and Mussels 36

     Clementine 38

The G7 Chord...40

     Aloha 'Oe...41

     When the Saints Go Marching In.........42

     Love Somebody.................................43

     The Streets of Laredo.........................44

The Down-and-Up Stroke 45

The G Chord...46

The D7 Chord...46

   Calypso Strum 47

Introducing F-Sharp.....................................47

     Sloop John B........................................48

SELECTING YOUR UKULELE

DO IT YOURSELF: UKULELE

Ukuleles come in different types and sizes. There are four basic sizes: soprano, concert, tenor, and baritone. The smallest is the soprano, and they get gradually larger, with the baritone being the largest.

Soprano   **Concert**   **Tenor**   **Baritone**

Soprano, concert, and tenor ukuleles are all tuned to the same notes, but the baritone is tuned differently. Each ukulele has a different sound. The soprano has a light, soft sound, which is what you expect when you hear a ukulele. The larger the instrument, the deeper the sound is. Some tenor ukuleles have six or even eight strings.

The soprano ukulele is the most common, but you can use soprano, concert, and four-string tenor ukuleles with this book. Because the baritone ukulele is tuned to the same notes as the top four strings of the guitar, you can use *Learn to Play the Alfred Way: Baritone Uke* (#380) to start learning how to play the baritone ukulele.

THE PARTS OF YOUR UKULELE

DO IT YOURSELF: UKULELE

Headstock

Tuning Pegs

Nut

Fret

Fingerboard

Soundhole

Bridge

HOW TO HOLD YOUR UKULELE

DO IT YOURSELF: UKULELE

Standing

Cradle the ukulele with your right arm by gently holding it close to your body. Your right hand should be free to strum it. Keep your left wrist away from the fingerboard. This allows your fingers to be in a better position to finger the chords.

Sitting

Rest the ukulele gently on your thigh.

THE RIGHT HAND: STRUMMING THE STRINGS
DO IT YOURSELF: UKULELE

 To *strum* means to play the strings with your right hand by brushing quickly across them. There are two common ways of strumming the strings. One is with a pick, and the other is with your fingers.

Strumming with a Pick

Hold the pick between your thumb and index finger. Hold it firmly, but don't squeeze it too hard.

Strum from the 4th string (closest to the ceiling) to the 1st string (closest to the floor).

Important: Always strum by mostly moving your wrist, not just your arm. Use as little motion as possible. Start as close to the top strings as you can, and never let your hand move past the edge of the ukulele.

Start near the top string.

Move mostly your wrist, not just your arm. Finish near the bottom string.

Strumming with Your Fingers

Decide if you feel more comfortable strumming with the side of your thumb or the nail of your index finger. The strumming motion is the same with the thumb or finger as it is when using the pick. Strum from the 4th string to the 1st string.

Strumming with the thumb.

Strumming with the index finger.

USING YOUR LEFT HAND

DO IT YOURSELF: UKULELE

Hand Position

Learning to use your left-hand fingers starts with a good hand position. Place your hand so your thumb rests comfortably in the middle of the back of the neck. Position your fingers on the front of the neck as if you are gently squeezing a ball between them and your thumb. Keep your elbow in and your fingers curved.

Keep elbow in and fingers curved.

Like gently squeezing a ball between your fingers and thumb.

Finger numbers.

Placing a Finger on a String

When you press a string with a left-hand finger, make sure you press firmly with the tip of your finger and as close to the fret wire as you can without actually being right on it. Short fingernails are important! This will create a clean, bright tone.

RIGHT
Finger pressing the string down near the fret without actually being on it.

WRONG
Finger is too far from fret wire; tone is "buzzy" and indefinite.

WRONG
Finger is on top of fret wire; tone is muffled and unclear.

HOW TO TUNE YOUR UKULELE

DO IT YOURSELF: UKULELE

Make sure your strings are wound properly around the tuning pegs. They should go from the inside to the outside, as in the picture below.

Tuning a tuning peg clockwise makes the pitch lower. Turning a tuning peg counterclockwise makes the pitch higher. Be sure not to tune the strings too high because they could break!

higher   higher

3rd String C   2nd String E

lower   lower

4th String G   1st String A

Important:

Always remember that the string closest to the floor is the 1st string. The one closest to the ceiling is the 4th string.

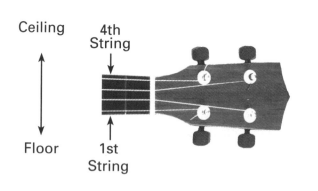

Ceiling   4th String

Floor   1st String

Tuning with the Online Media

When tuning while watching the online media, listen to the directions and match each of your ukulele's strings to the corresponding pitches on the online media.

Tuning the Ukulele to Itself

When your 1st string is in tune, you can tune the rest of the strings just using the ukulele alone.
If you have a piano or keyboard available, then tune the 1st string to A on the piano, and then follow the instructions below to get the ukulele in tune.

Press fret 5 of string 2 and tune it to the pitch of string 1 (A).

Press fret 4 of string 3 and tune it to the pitch of string 2 (E).

Press fret 2 of string 4 and tune it to the pitch of string 1 (A).

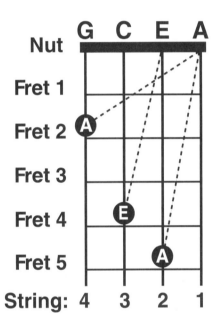

Pitch Pipes and Electronic Tuners

If you don't have a piano available, buying an electronic tuner or pitch pipe is recommended. The salesperson at your local music store can show you how to use them.

Musical sounds are indicated by symbols called *notes*. Their time value is determined by their color (white or black) and by stems or flags attached to the note.

Head ←

← **Stem**

← **Flag**

The Staff

The notes are named after the first seven letters of the alphabet (A–G), repeated to embrace the entire range of musical sound. The name and pitch of the note is determined by its position on the *staff*, which is made up of five horizontal lines and the spaces between.

5th LINE

4th LINE — 4th SPACE

3rd LINE — 3rd SPACE

2nd LINE — 2nd SPACE

1st LINE — 1st SPACE

Notes on the lines — Notes in the spaces

E G B D F   F A C E

Measures

Music is divided into equal parts called *measures*. One measure is divided from another by a *bar line*.

Bar lines

Measure — Measure

Clefs

During the evolution of musical notation, the staff had from 2 to 20 lines, and symbols were invented to locate certain lines and the pitch of the note on that line. These symbols are called *clefs*.

Music for ukulele is written in the *G clef,* or *treble clef*. Originally, the Gothic letter G was used on a four-line staff to establish the pitch of G.

This grew into the modern notation:

G

READING TAB
DO IT YOURSELF: UKULELE

All the music in this book is written two ways: in standard music notation and TAB.

Below each standard music staff, you'll find a four-line TAB staff. Each line represents a string of the ukulele, with the 1st string at the top and the 4th string at the bottom.

— 1st string
— 2nd string
— 3rd string
— 4th string

Numbers placed on the TAB lines tell you which fret to play. A **0** means to play the string open (not fingered).

| 1st string 3rd fret | 2nd string 1st fret | 3rd string open | 4th string open |

By glancing at the TAB, you can immediately tell where to play a note. Although you can't tell exactly what the rhythm is from the TAB, the horizontal spacing of the numbers gives you a strong hint about how long or short the notes are to be played.

CHORD DIAGRAMS
DO IT YOURSELF: UKULELE

Chord diagrams are used to indicate fingering for chords. The example to the right means to place your 1st finger on the 1st fret, 1st string, then strum all four strings. The o symbols on the 2nd, 3rd, and 4th strings indicate to play them open (not fingered).

Strings: 4th 3rd 2nd 1st

THE FIRST STRING A

DO IT YOURSELF: UKULELE

OPEN STRING
(not fingered)

2nd FRET

3rd FRET

A   B   C

Play slowly and evenly. Use only down-strokes, indicated by ⊓. Remember, the symbol ○ over a note means *open string*. Do not finger.

PLAYING WITH A, B, AND C

USED TO SIGNAL THE END OF THE PIECE

12

EXTRA CREDIT

Make sure to place your left-hand fingers as close to the fret wires as possible without touching them. When you play the B on the 2nd fret and follow it with the C on the 3rd fret, keep your 2nd finger down. You will only hear the C, but when you go back to the B, it will sound smooth.

SOUND-OFF: HOW TO COUNT TIME
DO IT YOURSELF: UKULELE

Four Kinds of Notes

QUARTER NOTE
ONE COUNT
COUNT: 1 2 3 4

HALF NOTE
TWO COUNTS
COUNT: 1 2 3 4

DOTTED HALF NOTE
THREE COUNTS
COUNT: 1 2 3

WHOLE NOTE
FOUR COUNTS
COUNT: 1 2 3 4

Time Signatures

Each piece of music has numbers at the beginning called a *time signature*. These numbers tell us how to count time. The TOP NUMBER tells us how many counts are in each measure. The BOTTOM NUMBER tells us what kind of note gets one count.

FOUR COUNTS TO A MEASURE

A QUARTER NOTE GETS ONE COUNT

THREE COUNTS TO A MEASURE

A QUARTER NOTE GETS ONE COUNT

TWO COUNTS TO A MEASURE

A QUARTER NOTE GETS ONE COUNT

Important: Go back and fill in the missing time signatures of the songs already learned.

REPEAT SIGNS

DO IT YOURSELF: UKULELE

This music uses *repeat signs*. The double dots inside the double bars tell you that everything in between those double bars is to be repeated.

The best way to learn all the songs and exercises is to listen to the recording first so that you can hear exactly what is going to happen. Follow along in the music as you listen. Then, enjoy playing along.

1ST STRING BLUES

THE SECOND STRING E
DO IT YOURSELF: UKULELE

 OPEN STRING

  1st FRET

  3rd FRET

E   F   G

FRET 1
FRET 2
FRET 3

Count: 1   2   3   4   1   2   3   4   (etc.)

```
0 0 0 0 | 1 1 1 1 | 3 3 3 3 | 1 1 1 1
```

```
0  0  1  1 | 3  3  1  1 | 0  1  3  1 | 0  3  0  0
```

 # JAMMIN' ON TWO STRINGS

Count: 1   2   3   4   (etc.)

```
0  1  3  0 |  0  2  3  0  |  0  1  3  0 |  3  2  0  3
```

```
0  1  3  0 |  0  2  3  0  3  2  0 |  3  0  1  1  1
```

HOT CROSS BUNS

18

BLUES IN C

If you have a friend or teacher and he or she wants to play along with you, the chord symbols above each staff may be used for a teacher-student duet. These chords are not to be played by the student.

ROCKIN' UKE

THE THIRD STRING C
DO IT YOURSELF: UKULELE

OPEN STRING

2nd FRET

C

D

JAMMIN' ON THREE STRINGS

LARGO
from the *New World Symphony*

Antonín Dvořák

JINGLE BELLS

BEAUTIFUL BROWN EYES

TEACHER: C

INTRODUCING B-FLAT
DO IT YOURSELF: UKULELE

A *flat* ♭ lowers a note a half step. B♭ is played one fret lower than the note B. When a flat note appears in a measure, it is still flat until the end of that measure.

1st FRET

B♭

 ## AURA LEE

This old American folk song was later recorded by Elvis Presley and called "Love Me Tender."

New Note B♭

THREE-STRING BOOGIE

This song uses all the notes you have learned. Don't forget to listen to the MP3 audio or DVD first!

TEMPO SIGNS
DO IT YOURSELF: UKULELE

A *tempo sign* tells you how fast to play the music. Below are the three most common tempo signs, which are Italian words. In some music, you will see tempo signs written in English.

Andante ("ahn-DAHN-teh") means to play slow.

Moderato ("moh-deh-RAH-toh") means to play moderately.

Allegro ("ah-LAY-groh") means to play fast.

Quarter Rest

This sign indicates silence for one count. For a clearer effect, you may stop the sound of the strings by touching the strings lightly with the heel of the right hand.

 THREE-TEMPO ROCKIN' UKE

Play three times: first time **Andante**, second time **Moderato**, third time **Allegro**.

THE C7 CHORD

o = open string

- - - - - - - - - = string is not played

Place your 1st finger in position, then play one string at a time.

Play all four strings together:

 + + + =

C⁷ Chord

Play slowly and evenly. Each slash mark / means to repeat the previous chord. Strum downward for each chord name and slash mark. Use your finger or a pick. The chord name is repeated in each measure.

28

THE F CHORD
DO IT YOURSELF: UKULELE

Place your 1st and 2nd fingers in position, then play one string at a time.

Play all four strings together:

 + + + =

F Chord

1. F / | F / | F / | F / | F / | F / ‖

2. F / / | F / / | F / / | F / / ‖

3. F / / / | F / / / | F / / / ‖

Once you can play both the F and C7 chords clearly, try combining them as in the following exercises.

1. F / / / | F / / / | C⁷ / / / | C⁷ / / / | F / / / | C⁷ / / / | F / / / | F ‖
HOLD

2. F / / | F / / | C⁷ / / | C⁷ / / | F / / | C⁷ / / | F / / | F 𝄽 𝄽 ‖
COUNT: 1 REST REST

3. F / | F / | C⁷ / | C⁷ / | F / | C⁷ / | F / | F / ‖

GOOD NIGHT LADIES

For this song and most of the rest of the songs in this book, you can play either the melody or chords. Your teacher can play the part you aren't playing, or you can play along with the MP3 audio or DVD.

Moderato

KEY SIGNATURES
DO IT YOURSELF: UKULELE

The *key signature* at the beginning of a piece tells you when a note is played as a flat note throughout the piece. In "Down in the Valley," each B is played as B-flat.

Ties

This curved line is called a *tie*. It connects two or more notes and ties them together. Play or sing the note once and hold it for the value of both (or more) tied notes.

In TAB, a tied note is shown as a number in parentheses. Do not pick the note again.

DOWN IN THE VALLEY

Key Signature: remember to play each B one half step lower.

ODE TO JOY
Theme from Beethoven's *Ninth Symphony*

Moderato

THE C CHORD

DO IT YOURSELF: UKULELE

Place your 3rd finger in position, then play one string at a time.

Play all four strings together:

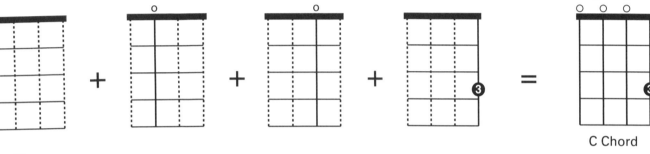

C Chord

Play slowly and evenly.

Now try these exercises. They combine all the chords you know.

1. 2/4 C / | C / | C⁷ / | C⁷ / | F / | F / | C / | C / ‖

2. 3/4 F / / | C / / | F / / | C⁷ / / | F / / | F 𝄽 𝄽 ‖

3. 4/4 C / / / / | C⁷ / / / / | F / / / / | C / / / / | F / / / / | C / / / / | C / / / / ‖

INCOMPLETE MEASURES

Not all pieces of music begin on the first beat. Sometimes, music begins with an incomplete measure called a *pickup*. If the pickup is one beat, often the last measure will only have three beats in $\frac{4}{4}$, or two beats in $\frac{3}{4}$.

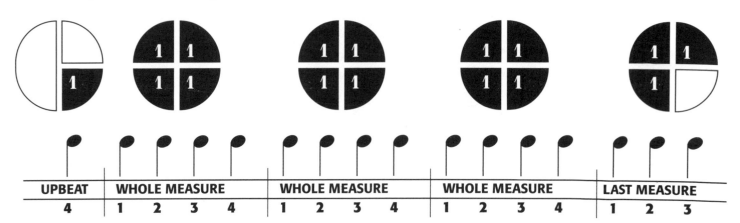

UPBEAT	WHOLE MEASURE	WHOLE MEASURE	WHOLE MEASURE	LAST MEASURE
4	1 2 3 4	1 2 3 4	1 2 3 4	1 2 3

A-TISKET, A-TASKET

EIGHTH NOTES
DO IT YOURSELF: UKULELE

Eighth notes are black notes that have a flag added to the stem: ♪ or ♫.

Two or more eighth notes are written with a *beam*: ♫ or ♫. Each eighth note receives one half beat.

| WHOLE NOTE | 2 HALF NOTES | 4 QUARTER NOTES | 8 EIGHTH NOTES |

Use alternating down-strokes ⊓ and up-strokes V on eighth notes.

COUNT: 1 & 2 & 3 & 4 & 1 & 2 & 3 & 4 &

JAMMIN' WITH EIGHTH NOTES

Allegro moderato*

*Allegro moderato means moderately fast.

DOTTED QUARTER NOTES
DO IT YOURSELF: UKULELE

A dot increases the length of a note by one half.

 Preparatory Drill

The only difference in the following two measures and those directly above them is the way they are written. They should sound the SAME.

 COCKLES AND MUSSELS

CLEMENTINE

lost and gone for - ev - er; Dread-ful sor - ry, Clem-en - tine.

ADDITIONAL VERSES

Verse 2:
Light she was and like fairy,
And her shows were number nine,
Herring boxes without topses,
Sandals were for Clementine

Chorus:
Oh my darlin', oh my darlin',
Oh my darlin', Clementine!
You are lost and gone forever
Dreadful sorry, Clementine.

Verse 3:
Drove she ducklings to the water
Every morning just at nine,
Hit her foot against a splinter,
Fell into the foaming brine.

Chorus:
Oh my darlin', oh my darlin'
Oh my darlin', Clementine!
You are lost and gone forever
Dreadful sorry, Clementine.

Verse 4:
Ruby lips above the water,
Blowing bubbles soft and fine,
But alas, I was no swimmer,
So I lost my Clementine.

Chorus:
Oh my darlin', oh my darlin'
Oh my darlin', Clementine
You are lost and gone forever,
Dreadful sorry, Clementine.

THE G7 CHORD
DO IT YOURSELF: UKULELE

Place your 1st, 2nd, and 3rd fingers in position, then play one string at a time.

Play all four strings together:

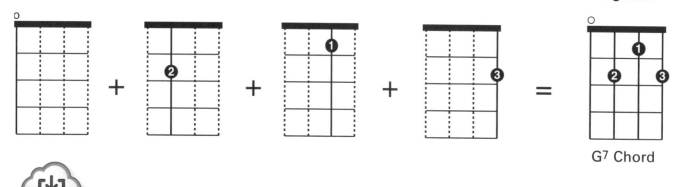

G7 Chord

Play slowly and evenly.

1. 4/4   G7 / / / | C / / / | G7 / / / | C / / / ||

2. 3/4   C / / | G7 / / | C / / | G7 / / | C / / | C 𝄽 𝄽 ||

3. 2/4   G7 / | C / | G7 / | C / | F / | C / | G7 / | C / ||

4. 4/4   C / / / | F / / / | C / / / | G7 / / / | C / / / | C / / 𝄽 ||

5. 3/4   C / / | C7 / / | F / / | C / / | F / / | F / / | C / / | C / / |

  G7 / / | G7 / / | C / / | F / / | C / / | C 𝄽 𝄽 ||

ALOHA 'OE
(Farewell to Thee)

To get used to playing the G7 chord, play this version of "Aloha 'Oe" (pronounced "oy") with just chords. Sing along with the melody.

This arrangement uses quarter-note slashes that indicate to play one strum on each quarter note.

Moderato

Fare - well to thee, Fare - well to

thee, O beau - teous one who lives a - mong the

flow - ers, one fond em - brace be -

fore I leave, un - til we

meet a - gain.

WHEN THE SAINTS GO MARCHING IN

LOVE SOMEBODY

THE STREETS OF LAREDO

Moderately

As I_____ walked out in the streets of La - re - do, as

I walked out in La - re - do one day, I

spied a young cow - boy all dressed in white lin - en, all

dressed in white lin - en as cold as the clay.

THE DOWN-AND-UP STROKE

DO IT YOURSELF: UKULELE

You can make your accompaniment of waltz songs in $\frac{3}{4}$ (like "The Streets of Laredo") more interesting by replacing the second beat of the measure with a down-stroke followed by an up-stroke. Together, the down-and-up strokes are played in the same time as a regular strum.

Try the following exercise to work on just the rhythm.

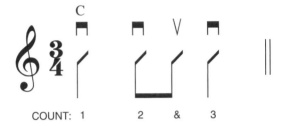

Now practice changing from C to G7.

Now practice changing back and forth from C to G7 and back. When you can do it smoothly, go back to page 44 and use it to accompany "The Streets of Laredo."

THE G CHORD
DO IT YOURSELF: UKULELE

Place your 1st, 2nd, and 3rd fingers in position, then play one string at a time.

Play all four strings together:

 + + + =

G Chord

THE D7 CHORD
DO IT YOURSELF: UKULELE

Place your 1st and 2nd fingers in position, then play one string at a time.

Play all four strings together:

 + + + =

D7 Chord

Calypso Strum

The calypso strum is used to accompany Caribbean songs like "Mary Ann," "Jamaica Farewell," and "Sloop John B." The rhythm is a little tricky, so make sure you can play the exercises on this page before trying the song on the following page.

Play a steady quarter-note pattern on a C chord. Use only down-strokes.

Now add an eighth note up-stroke after each down-stroke. Notice how the count has changed.

Now leave out the down-stroke on beat 3 and replace it with an eighth rest (𝄾) which is silent for half a beat. Notice that you now have two up-strokes in a row on the "and" of 2 and the "and" of 3.

This whole pattern represents one measure of the calypso strum. As soon as you can do it without missing a beat, try "Sloop John B."

INTRODUCING F-SHARP
DO IT YOURSELF: UKULELE

A *sharp* ♯ raises a note a half step. F♯ is played one fret higher than the note F. When a sharp note appears in a measure, it is still sharp until the end of that measure.

Notice "Sloop John B." on page 48 uses a key signature with one sharp. Key signatures can use either sharps or flats.

SLOOP JOHN B.

Start this song with the calypso strum to get into the rhythm of it. Then start singing.

Conclusion:

Congratulations, you have come a long way! You know the basics and played lots of fun songs. Continue learning more tunes and look for other musicians to play with as a duet or in a band. There is nothing better than jamming with others. Good luck!